COMPLICATED PLEASURES

First published in 2007
The Dedalus Press
13 Moyclare Road
Baldoyle
Dublin 13
Ireland

www.dedaluspress.com

ISBN 978 1 904556 75 6

Dedalus Press titles are represented in North America
by Syracuse University Press, Inc., 621 Skytop Road,
Suite 110, Syracuse, New York 13244, and in the UK by Central
Books, 99 Wallis Road, London E9 5LN

Printed and bound in the UK by Lightning Source, 6 Precedent
Drive, Rooksley, Milton Keynes MK13 8PR, UK

Typesetting: Pat Boran
Cover image: *Icarus 96*
by John Kelly (1932—2006), RHA

The Dedalus Press receives financial assistance from
An Chomhairle Ealaíon / The Arts Council, Ireland

COMPLICATED PLEASURES

Billy Ramsell

ACKNOWLEDGEMENTS

Acknowledgement is due to the editors of the following, in which a number of these poems, or versions of them, originally appeared:

Cork Literary Review, Magma, The Shop, Southword, The Stinging Fly and *The Sunday Tribune* (New Irish Writing).

Contents

To Dolly and Joan

1

Breath

These are the fragile hours, the bird-dominated silent hours
dawn is too simple a word for.

This Sunday morning light is pearl-pale and fragile,
revealing the almost empty quay,
the gulls that spire from the river to feast on Saturday night's debris,

a drowsy street-sweeper and me and you
standing almost still on a foot bridge
as we stare into the mussicating, stout-black Lee.

Because keeping schtum was never my strong point
I can't resist wanting
to stain this silence.

But as I draw breath to speak,
as I inhale one waft of this sweet dirty morning,
I remember Flaubert's lament
that language is a broken inadequate thing,
a toddler's tune played on pots and pans,

and how he saw through the troubadours'
claims to praise
something apart from their own serenades
that drifted up like balloons to the balconies.

So how can I exalt you with a few litres of air?

With this breath I could sketch some things for you:
children gathering stones on a beach in September,
plucking only the smooth, rounded ones
from the infinitely varied layer

that conceals the sand like a second skin,
like damp, beautiful scales.

But I know you'll know that's just faction.
And even if it were true,
it says more about me that it does about you.

Or I could make an air out of this breath,
slot my thoughts into some melody and sing:

Lady take my hand
and walk me through this sleeping world,
past South Gate Bridge, down French's Quay
where the morning has unfurled

the cathedral spires that echo
the brewery's oversized urns,
and the greasy pigeons settle
on every puddle that burns

magenta outside the funeral home
where the lisping river swerves
in an elbow-bend...

But no.

Whatever tune I ventured would be second-hand,
a standard thing you've heard before
my words must be squeezed into
and, besides, as you know too well I cannot sing.

Or with this breath I could launch into a list again,
exhale in service of the detail,
mention your remedies, your autumn sweater,
the wooden room in which you live

where I have been woken by your heart's easy rhythm,
or declare that the healthy part of you outweighs
my own unhealthy part.
(But that's just me talking about me again).

I could say your hair is honey
and your skin a sweeter, more translucent honey,
but your flesh, your complexity,
will succumb to description
no more than these slime-black river walls
to the swellings and recessions
of the river's mumbling slurp,

and whatever lines I shape with this breath
will scramble in air
like these greedy, hunting gulls
and circle your beauty
but never alight perfectly on you.

Before this weary, new, hungover world
tilts another few degrees, I will unleash
this breath into the morning I snatched it from,
not as praise or recollection
or some desperate plea,
but into your own mouth,
and I will taste the air
that has made your lungs swell,
flooding their intricate networks
down to the forested alveoli,
that has sampled the intimate capillaried dark
no-one can ever know,
that tastes as your kisses tasted
when you kissed me dozens of times before,
of millet, alfalfa, rosemary, and yarrow,
of bread and lemon,
of salt or banana or of the night before.

Tomorrow, she whispered

You are beautiful as you are
because you do not know that you are beautiful.
For the gifts offered in ignorance
are the ones that sustain.

Take this rain through which we drunkenly dance:
what does it know of us, or of a busker's drunken tune?
Still it drenches us gently,
glittering in the dusk and under streetlights.
And if it stopped
what would we have to dance through?

Take this singer howling for coins:
what do his stumbling fingers know
when they fill the square with sound
of our sweet fear
as we dance round and round
the edge of something new?
Still they slide and fumble
and anger the frets to noise.

These things—'streetlights', 'guitar' and 'rain'—
what do they know of the names we have for them
or that we name them at all?
Still they offer themselves day after day
for the naming, making poems possible,
and enter them gently, uncertainly,
just as your life enters mine.

You are a little like the sun.
What does it know of heat, or distance,
or those of us, addicted to light, who depend on it?
So take this rain, take this singer,
take these things we have done, and have not done.
With your ignorant beauty, you are a little like the sun
that burns for me maybe
or maybe just for everyone.

Middle Distance

Strange Intimacies
and *Love's Treadmill: Romance in the Post-Human Epoch*
are the titles of two books I will never write
about the hours we spent jogging by the river.

When the factories sparkled on the estuary's far-side,
showering the water
with the glitter of night-shifts and sleepless machines

we huffed and puffed through the melting twilight,
trundled through bushes as the gravel whispered
and the chalk dust flew in the August air,
with steady acceleration we moved through those lane-ways
tangled with brambles and heavy with scent
as the jogger's monotonous elation came over us.

'This is so much nicer than the gym', you panted,
'that mucid air, the endless treadmill, MTV,
all that staring into the mirrors' middle distance.'
At some moist, heaving version of yourself
straining against the glass, sprinting for the world,
to be spat, drenched and uncertain, into existence.

I picked up the pace as the evening wilted
but you stayed on my shoulder only inches behind.

This, jogging together, is the strangest intimacy
when our breathing harmonises
and our rhythms mingle
in a fugue of breath,
and the sweat sprays
from our bodies as they heave in tandem.

But it can't last. After our sprint finish,
when you leaned on me and I was breathing
sea-salt from your beach-brown skin
and from your hair some clammy tang,

I realised you would always be somewhere
in the middle-distance,
that I could no more reach you
than I could my reflection in the gym's mirror,
that I could repeat these steps forever and never come close.

                    *

I looked out at the nitrified river,
at the bubbles popping gently on its agitated surface
until my breath came back.

Finding Touch

As the floodlights faded at Thomond
on a meaningless pre-season friendly,
and the Limerick mist stole down from the stands
like the ghost of a pitch-invasion

I thought of us.

For conscience is a whistle
you and I can barely hear
when the binding is complete
and we are perfectly intertwined,
rucking and scrummaging,
face to face or cheek
to sweat-soaked cheek.

And tell me this:
who enforces the laws of love,
those regulations that mutate and multiply
from season to season
without warning or explanation,
as we compete with each other tirelessly
for every inch of territory, of space?

Which is why I see us as two old pros
in some decayed provincial ground,
crouched and holding, heaving each other
back and forth across the gain line,
back and forth
over those hard-fought threadbare yards

until they turn the floodlights off,
until grass reclaims the terraces,
until the ref is a skeleton,
until we've both forgotten the rules
and what it is we're here for
and if what we're playing is a game.

The Connoisseur

When it came to happiness she was a gourmet,
a connoisseur of small moments and extravagance.
Like a hummingbird, free as jazz, she floated away.

She wasn't immune to love. But her need to stay
on top of things meant she didn't rate romance
when it came to happiness. She was a gourmet

of the ungraspable now, savouring on the spot, without delay,
what the rest of us reheat at a bitter distance.
Like a hummingbird, free as jazz, she floated away.

I envied her of course, which isn't to say
her dance, her casual way, didn't leave me in a trance.
When it came to happiness she was a gourmet.

To recognise contentment was her gift, her forte,
sipping the nectar from selected instants
like a hummingbird. Free as jazz, she floated away

from me with the old line: *Is there anything I can say
to make this easier for you?* Not a chance.
When it came to happiness she was a gourmet.
Like a hummingbird, free as jazz, she floated away.

Waking from the dream she visited

My eyes opened.
I gained the whole world
and lost you.

November will come

This is no season of the quartered orange,
squirting and splitting in your exquisite fingers.

Like the leaves.
You've gone,
like the carbon-dusted yellow leaves.

Last night I dreamt of the dark dogs
nuzzling and tearing at the refuse sacks
that languished in doorways,
and bled when slit open.

I am hunched in the laptop's glow.
Behind its hum
I can hear them now in the frozen streets beyond my window,

their whispers drifting through the alley ways
their claws clicking on the footpath.

2

The Magic Carpet

Because I am the greatest in his realm
your husband sent for me, left me alone with you in the inner palace

where, on pain of death, no man may tread.
My commission was to render your face

in silks and thread of gold, the most delicate of textiles.
Of course the inevitable happened (for the rumours

of your beauty weren't exaggerated) and I set out to make
                                                          your portrait
unfinishable. Every night I heard the women and eunuchs murmur

in the corridors: 'Hush, hush, the master is working!'
while every night my work was withering,

stitch by ripped stitch, in my own hands. How long can I explain
                                                          the delay,
my doings and undoings, this 'Penelopian' dithering?

Your face shimmers on the floor beneath me.
I cannot insert the final threads of jade and blue

for fear that we lift off before I can even step aside
and it carries me away from you.

Gift

If I ever encounter the Muse face to face,
in this world, or the next, or some state in between,

I'll say to her: 'though you are so often silent,
though you come to me, when you come at all,

disguised in so many wigs and skins,
and with different names, though most of the time

you ignore me I have kept this for you'.
And on my knees before her throne everlasting

I'll offer my gift: a paper-thin mirror,
frameless and frangible, silvered over

a thousand lunch breaks, Sundays, snatched half-hours,
that despite my best efforts is blurred and uneven.

But maybe, just maybe, she'll be startled to see
not just herself when she looks in its surface, but also

the bottle-nosed dolphin, *Tursiops truncatus,*
night-swimming through the estuary, an arc of muscle

shattering the starlight into miniature supernovae
the water's dying ripples heal again.

Poem

I waited ten years for her beauty
in this house I built by the water,
gave up my career, forgot my duty
to my son, to my unborn daughter.

The nights when she came smelled like nectar;
I sang her flowers, kissed her sweet tears.
There were other nights. I recollect
the endless waiting, the cold bed, the years.

So long...Where is the rest of my life?
I cannot imagine the face of my daughter.
I will wander the roads in search of my wife,
my son who calls another man 'father'.

A Supper Feast

after the Diaries *of Kenneth Williams*

There's just about time to hoover the lounge,
lay out my pills, to roast, with a little dill, a mutton joint,

to take in The News, feed my mother,
to write in my journal *What's the bloody point?*

And was it the needling lust for applause
or my fear of the sweat-streaked navvies, of myself,

that whittled my life to a series of sketches, that shackled me
morning and night to a limp-wristed prancing elf?

I can already see the too-short obituaries:
'Aged camp comedian…Spartan apartment'. You know the rest.

Forgive, forgive, is my advice, as much as you can.
I felt my heart rot like an apple in my chest

till it pumped only bitterness through me, till…Enough.
I want to think of boys, Moroccan light, my occasional excesses.

My back aches. Which hurt me more,
my friends' failures, or their successes?

Four Darks in Red

after Mark Rothko

It was an aching for clarity that forced him to abandon
mid-winter and the flight of swallows,
sunlight, snow.

It was his refusal of geometry and a turn in the road,
of the oddness and perfection
of bodies

And his hatred of accident,
of the thing out of place,
of the *thing*

That caused him to vanish in painting,
to generate fishless shimmering
oceans,

To fold the world like a tent
and carry it after him
into the canvas

And to let the whole lot dissolve;
even himself, skin and hair
and bone and balls

And leave only an agitated surface
an empty red

Sea that seethes gleaming
lusting

To consume

Itself

With Summer Come the Flies

to Louise

The world was mellowing and turning gold.

Relishing pints, the first sip's fizzing bitterness
             and the black surge dousing the throat,

we sat near the window in McCarthy's bar

savouring the hangover-soothing smell of fish,
washes of sun-haze touching the water

             and the clouds, cobwebs in a sun-filled attic,
             complex, light-kissed, and infinitely fragile.

They say we shouldn't look for analogues in nature
but who can blame me for seeing our lives in those clouds?
For even then, teeth-deep in the ripening afternoon,
I realised how vulnerable and strange and one-off
our hours together were,
that our lives are sculpted like clouds in the wind
by lust and departures and failure and love,
the bomb, the built-in obsolescence of the species,
that life without Lou was just round the corner,
         an end to driving westward, to nothing to do,
         to Miles Davis's *Kind of Blue*,
         to Beck, to Bach, to Leonard Cohen,
         to Bonny Billy, to Nina Simone,
         to George's Quay and foot massages, to the picture you drew
         of me unawares smoking the herb, to medicine, the
                            Malaysian crew,
         to Rory's sculpture, Steve's guitar, Django's 'Blue Drag',

to us crossing half of Europe to meet you in Prague
(at 4pm on the 4th of September
a rendezvous you were certain we'd never remember),
to the lazy summers that so sneakily flew,
to hours of stargazing, flat on our backs in my back garden,
                                            wet with dew,
to College road, to Dutch Gold, to 'six-for-a-fiver',
to hours of gazing at the river
groping its drunken meander through UCC,
to Murphy's, Black Russians, G and T,
to An Bróg, The Oval, The Gateway Bar,
An Spailpín Fánach, to the life-restoring 'Sunday jar',
to the hangover soothing smell of coffee
in Bica on a Sunday morning, to scrambled eggs, banoffi,
croissants, ciabatta, chicken tikka,
to the sad, antiseptic ghost-ridden shell that's all that's left
                                            of the Bica,
that our lives, our friendships, our sturdiest loves are no
                                            more solid or stable
than this already-vanishing never to be repeated now at this table,
than this tang of stout on my tongue,
than this delicate flake of cloud, than this cloud-filtered
                                            spillage of sun,
than this woven, reworked and rewoven poem
that is home
for a moment to this precious few; than this precious few:
Brian and Rhona, and Billy and Gavin, and Bar and Lou.

All things must pass, the old masters tell us,

I took my glass and sank the bitter dregs,

and suddenly drunk and bitter walked out along the pier

and searched for a poem, a formula of words,

to make it all as transparent, and recurring, and uncomplicated,
              as the sunlight, in dying slants caressing the water,

      as the water, viscous, thick with light,
              lustral, murmuring, amber.

An Otter

Christmas day, 4 O'clock,
Stumps of cloud, like yellowing tower blocks,
Lean over
The failing glimmer of Christmas lights
And the quays, utterly empty,

Except

For one dark otter, slick with river slime,

A shape

Made of dark Lee water,
Of thick fluid,
Of rippling muscle,

Swaggering, like any pedestrian,
Up the steps from the riverbed,
Across the street,
Past dim shop displays, shuttered windows,

Toward an empty car askew on the footpath,
Its engine idling, its front door open,
Its headlights ploughing the gloom,

And a girl, its driver,
Standing alone on the pavement.

Innocent, beautiful.
She leans over the otter,
Her long hair hanging down

As a second slinks up
The steps from the riverbed,
Like a hand sliding slowly
From a hip to a breast.

El Raval

It is evening and the light grows indolent.
It mooches through the streets of Raval,
through *Calle Tallers* and *Hospital,*

past a babble of Spaniards
and the svelte Nigerian whores that appear
—like night solidifying—on the fringes of the *Ramblas,*

it limps past the curry houses and the Asian stores,
past the Algerians, thin as flick-knives,
that linger in doorways.

It sidles into a yellowing bar
and settles a moment on sweating *tortilla,*
on the squat barman

swabbing his counter at the end of his day,
on leather-skinned gents
bent above chessboards and pale *con leche.*

It reveals the ornate corner table,
where a skinny boy sits
with his notebook open, writing:

There was snow on palm trees
on Rambla Raval. ~~That day we came back from~~.
Delicately frosted fronds.

~~Rich and~~. How startling, to me,
that combination. ~~Juxtapo~~.
Like when you speak one language and then another.

36

Then, like grey water down a plughole,
the worn-out, lazy light of evening
vanishes—swirling—into his eye

as he closes his notebook,
leaves a modest tip for the barman
and strolls out past the muttering regulars

to the *Calle's* irriguous twilight,
to Indian smells, mosque-bound Moroccans
and ragged art students,

to jazz slouching from an open bar
that mingles with the *adhan*
and floats upwards

into the dusky, lascivious sky—
a black whore arching
its back over the *barrio*.

From Mutton Lane

The fish scents are missing your nostrils again.

The hake
and bream smells
   slip
      away

from the fish stalls

and meander
            through the market

      in search of
                  you

            through
the bustling odours of the olive and cheese stalls

past Mr Bell's
   and the Chicken Inn
      past Bresnan's
         the Chocolate Shop
         and Durcan's

                  into

                  stained sunlight, into Mutton Lane,
                  keg-smells and fag-tangs, oblivion.

I have folded this page round marennes and whitstables
then sent it to Tyneside

so that when you slit the envelope open
        their oyster scents

                up coil and
            rise   collect
        might   themselves

            before crashing your sino-nasal cavity

            like a breaker flooding a notched cave near Ballycotton
                        in a gulch-flushing
                    surge

                    up
                    tunnels

                        to a silent, dripping centre

                a climbing wave
                salty, ravenous

Skiing with Zuzana

I have a box full of poems about whiteness
but only one that tells a story of happiness,

which is the poem, Zuzana, you're reading now,
settling on this page like blackbirds on the snow

you brought me to in south-eastern Germany
where you and father tried to teach me how to ski.

I could only look at you and laugh, Ms Hrabetova,
as your skis caressed the mountain like a lover

but even I managed once to cleave the air,
almost before I knew it, in a slant of laughing terror

as my mass transformed to movement with a stroke.
Don't cross the skis, Bill, break, break!

I was flat on my ass in my borrowed gear
for the thirty-fifth time when there they were:

a cluster of cobalt weeds in a tree-crevice,
their lavender fragility crisped with ice.

Each stem and petal seemed to blur, to float
outside itself, like the colours Novalis sought.

Their phylum, species, genus I don't know,
being expert neither with flowers nor snow

but they were basic and renewable, had witnessed dew
and storms and their afterglow and I wanted to pick them for you.

But something about their feat
of bleak survival made me hesitate.

They were the mountain's gift to us, to tell us we were loved
and sheltered by its vastness. They should not be removed

as badge for lapel, trophy for buttonhole or well-meant token,
but left for those shapely frauleins, the nimble children

who coast down the slope in bobble-hats and Spandex,
each piece of gleaming kit exquisitely and visibly branded.

Those weeds would be a renewable blue resource
if I let them be, but in our hands they would die within hours.

I did not take them in your father's glove.
For words are like this. It is the tiny ones I love.

Blooming on street corners, suspended in the ice
of dictionaries, they survive beneath our notice,

flourish in the language quietly, decline and grow,
renew themselves each summer like flowers after snow.

But because you taught me how to ski, and because I know,
deep down, that your mind is clean as snow

only for you, Zuz, would I break each stem
and make them rhyme. For who else would I disturb them?

While You Were Out

I managed a last nuchal kiss
as she eased herself out of the bed.

She half-turned with a half-smile
and sank her hands in her hair.

(You were browsing the market, at that very moment,
in search of dragon-fruit and ashwaganda).

Through the gapped curtains
a tongue of sunlight
caressed her curiously dimpled ass,
her yellow knickers.

It lambently licked the lamina of sweat on her back.

It kissed the bronze froth that fell to her shoulders,
her face in quarter profile

(that face which so many others had touched,
the flops, the forgotten and the canonised)

as she suddenly, somehow, became thin and shimmering,
her body, it seemed, transformed to heat haze.

She flickered for a long moment
like the flimsiest mirage,
smiled that thin smile

and was gone
as if she'd been beamed up or evaporated.

I was left with nothing but the mangled bedclothes,
the carpet, the wardrobe
you'd transplanted from your childhood bedroom,

the desk with my open notebook
and the picture of the two of us in San Moritz
(remember the huge Swede who snapped us?),
the dozing computer that hummed
the same note to itself over and over,

its gleaming curves
its screen on which these words
were blinking

3

Complicated Pleasures

We were in bed together listening to Lyric,
to a special about the Russians,
when the tanks rolled into Babylon.

For a second I could feel their engines,
and the desert floor vibrating
in the radio's bass rattling your bedroom
as the drums expanded at the centre of the *Leningrad,*
as those sinister cellos invaded the melody.

We'd been trying, for the hell of it,
to speak our own tongue
and I was banging on about Iberia when your eyelids closed:
'*Tá do lámh I mo lámh,*' I whispered, '*ar nós cathair bán
sna sléibhte lárnach, d'anáil ar nós suantraí na mara i mBarcelona.
Codhladh sámh.*'

But as I murmured 'sleep, my darling, sleep' into your sleeping ear
I found myself thinking of magnets,
of what I'd learned in school about the attraction of opposites,
that the two of us, so similar,
could only ever repel one another.

For the closer I clutched your compact body
the further we grew apart.

You have eleven laughs
and seven scents
and I know them like a language.
But what will it matter when the bombs start to fall
that you could never love me?

Then you turned in my arms
and it was midnight again on the beach at Ardmore,
when the starlight collected in some rock pool or rain pool
among the ragged crags at the water's edge
and the two of us sat there
and we didn't even breathe,
determined not to the disturb that puddle's flux,
the tiny light-show in its rippling shallows,
the miniature star-charts that for a moment inhabited it,

and you whispered that the planets, like us, are slaves to magnetism,
gravity's prisoners, as they dance the same circles
again and again, that even stars ramble mathematically,
their glitter preordained to the last flash.

You turned again as I looked at the night sky
through your attic window
and thought of the satellites
gliding and swivelling in their infinite silence,
as they gaze down on humanity's fumbling,
on you and me, as you sniffled against my neck
and the drumming, drumming flooded your bedroom,
on powerful men in offices pressing buttons
that push buttons in powerful men,
on the tanks, like ants, advancing through wilderness.

Those pitiless satellites, aware of every
coming conflagration and what would burn in it,
knowing for certain in their whispering circuits
that, like our island's fragile language,
like Gaudi's pinnacles and the *Leningrad* symphony,
—even worse—like your teeth and our four hands,
the very stars through which they wander
would be gone, those brittle constellations

with the billion sinners that orbit them,
extinguished in a heartbeat, instantly absolved,
as if your hand had brushed the water, slowly, once.

Scan

to Hannah

Invisible and gentle hands.

The waves of ultrasound
probe the womb you float in
and trace your shape on the printout
that slides like a tongue
from the whirring computerbank.

You're there in white, near actual size,
a podding blob against the blackness

that could be a new-spawned milky galaxy,
a spiral in the lens
of a mid-western radio-telescope

or an image of Baghdad from the night-bombing,
briefed on in Centcom,
snapped by a priceless bird set roaming
in fluid geosynchronous ovals.

But I want to think of you as Prague
glimpsed on a night-flight,
a city glittering with the flimsy light
of the million people you will not become
and the one, touch wood, you someday might

or as the moon in the river
under South Gate Bridge,
a bright, wrinkled disc upon the Beamish Lee.

You are a swirl of milk in a coffee cup,
the stuff that makes the dark stuff white.

In the Arab Barber's

Barcelona, 2001

In the Arab barber's, on *Calle Hospital,*
I sat in a row of dark-skinned others,

the air thick with consonants, dark and hard.
Wide-eyed with top-grade Moroccan, the two brothers

scissored and sheared. In the queue my place was skipped.
Hair collected on the dirty lino in small misshapen rodents.

I tried to ignore the washed-out faces, the lavish tracksuits,
the voices that seemed permanently raised in argument.

Acrid grass wafted from the backroom.
Longing for Spanish, I sat tight,

fidgeted with an incomprehensible magazine
(how do you read this stuff? right to left or left to right?)

till the Arab barber beckoned with a clanging monosyllable.
In the mirror left was right, and, as he stripped my three-day growth,

I could not judge the distance between us,
his shadowed eyes and mine, the blade and my proffered throat.

Still Life with Frozen Pizza

to Ger Gleeson

I unwrapped the plastic and slid the icy disc
onto the oven shelf. 15 minutes later, as the TV rippled

into wakefulness, the tray made a presentable still life:
the pizza's cracked lunar surface, its pepperoni nipples,

the burnt ridge round its edge, the remote
that liked to sit in my hand, snug as a gun

in its futuristic sleekness,
a phaser set permanently to stun.

I navigated *Countdown*, sitcoms, pantomime wrestling,
rolling news. Somewhere bombs were falling:

the crosshairs at the centre of the grainy video.
A building dissolved in dust, its crater spoiling

the streetscape's geometric perfection.
The next one, I thought, *will probably be pay-per-view.*

Full, I balked at the pizza's final quarter,
then pierced its plasticky skin with a spurt of goo.

A girl bawled at the camera, weary, untranslated,
a film of dirt on her denim, her face.

I popped the last cheese-string into my mouth, sat back
with a quiet burp of contentment, and flicked over to *Will & Grace*.

Monet's War

He must have known, when he chose to stay pottering
about that garden he'd managed to within a lily of perfection,

when he chose to stay painting instead of evacuating,
that the barbarians were only a few miles to the north.

One imagines he can hear the howitzers, throwing tantrum
after tantrum at the firmament, and smell the fields that are spongy

with the tissue and fluids of wheelwrights and dentists
dressed as soldiers, as he dodders over the Japanese bridge,

past azaleas and irises and a furnace of nasturtiums
to the lily-pond. Stubborn old man. Why does he keep on pouring

water into canvases and just stand there staring into them,
at marmalade water, pad-blobs, a lush and rippling turbulence?

Why shape each depthless surface of indulgence,
each oceanic vertical puddle, in the hour of the bayonet,

now gouache is impossible, now bi-planes clatter above the garden
and the second gardener has absconded south?

In Memory of Veronica Guerin

It matters what we journalists do.
If I didn't think my work made a difference,
I'd probably give it up.
—Veronica Guerin

She must have known. As the junkies squirmed out
like grubs from the tower-blocks, shuffling their sun-shy bodies

in search of gear and *Vienetta,* she'd drive down through
the tenements at evening, past betting-offices, past bars,

to hold hushed truck with murderers in the buildings' shadows.
They were shabby entrepreneurs, almost children,

with their ridiculous *Marvel*-ian sobriquets, Zombie and the Vampire,
with their contested tyrannies like patches of school-yard.

She must have known they were stupid and callous as children
when she wrote them and herself into her story all that damp year

mortality became penetrable and forbidding as police-tape.
As she continued to file dispatches from the land of shattered windows,

to traffic gossip, to shape—in installments—a teasing penny-dreadful,
she must have known about the indicator's tick-tock trochees

at the traffic-light, about the black bird taking wing from the
                                                    traffic-light,
about her glance into the rearview mirror at the motorbike

approaching through a grubby swirl of diesel fumes, into the sun,
into the shotgun's muzzle, its black-zero that was forever.

54

You and the Sea

In your dream I am driving (badly, as usual,
but stay calm) as we move eastward to the sea,

tracked by the gaze of speed cam and sat cam,
by the GPS devices in our mobile phones. Don' t worry,

my presence in your slumber is strictly short term,
I have nothing untoward in mind,

and, besides, your sleep was always shallow,
a trembling rockpool, you can wake up anytime.

Is this the ultimate invasion of your privacy,
to enter and manipulate the most intimate theatre

of your sleeping, to exercise the craft that lets
me script and cast your dreams like a director?

For those presences might have followed me
into your mind's inner chamber, those bodiless mainframes

that see so much of what we do in the world.
To think I might have led them into your dreams!

But because I know you will not come for me again
I had to turn up here, not to ask you for the second chance

it's not in your gift to give, and that I don't anyway want,
nor for forgiveness, nor for the complicated pleasure of your hands,

but for this: allow me sculpt your slumber
into something to remember me by. For the world we wake in

is a grove of worries: child care, your second job,
the bills your hungry letter-box takes in,

the alarm-clock perched upon your bedside table,
examining you all night with its red eyes,

rationing every numbered minute of the sleep
your brain craves. But let me exploit your dreams' flexibilities

and turn the few minutes before the clock goes off
into a lost weekend. I will set the sky to sun

and the season to July and turn up the sea's placidity.
I can conjure your choice of accommodation.

For two whole nights I will hear your breathing
and the sea and nothing else. We can wake and swim

for I want to see again the water lapping your hips
and belly, that negligible sliver, forming islands on the skin

between your breasts. And if I script a walk along the cliff together
will we see, out where the rabbits occasionally hide

in the overgrowth, an off-white butterfly fall on your hand
like an over-blown snowflake, or a rust-coloured butterfly

flame for you? Because I shape this dream
we can eat out at The Forge on almost anything:

bruscetta, yielding swordfish, lemon sole. But now
this dream must be brought to its ending

even before your alarm clock's whinny cuts through
the restaurant. Before they realise I'm here,

those digital minds evolved beyond silicone,
before they follow me into your slumber

with their eyes, with their fibre optics that are finer
than the finest hair on your daughter's head.

But wait! Before you wake let's quickly settle the bill,
even as the lime-green headland becomes suddenly fluid,

and the barnacled storm wall, and the sweltering tar
outside this brasserie that is about to ripple and dissolve

as the sea-noise turns into traffic, my hand on your back
into a bed-spring. and you're reeled up, upwards into yourself.

Silent Alarm

Feel that? One of those inexplicable shivers,
the flesh stretching at the base of your neck,
rippling in a wave-pattern?

You're being credit-checked
by a mainframe in Brussels.
Your girlfriend's sister's Googling you
in a Liverpool cybercafé.

A blackbird, in Waterford,
has alighted on your grave.

Sparkle

I am the extraneous star
in the constellation

you pointed out to your godson
last summer in Hastings.

I am a one-eyed God
adrift in the heavens,

assessing your overgrown puddles of light,
your rivers and troop movements with my lens

that keeps swivelling
as your image arrows into my brain

across the endless expanses of silent frigidity
from where you sit in the Co-op café

with that soft-covered book open on the tablecloth
beside your decaf latte and banoffi pie.

The night-sky is pristine beyond the listed windows.
Turn around. Look up. What am I?

Gated Community

He'd only stopped in for a capsicum, yoghurt, some duck liver pâté
when he saw it: *Protect yourself from identity theft!*

Keep sensitive personal info out of the wrong hands!
Somehow it ended up in his shopping basket.

That Thursday, bills ribboned into the Green bin.
Job done, he thought. Better safe than sorry.

Next week the device was next to the letterbox:
no sooner was the mail absorbed than he shredded it.

His wife chuckled. While she was out at the gym
he shredded her passport. An item a day, then two:

P45's and birth certificates, their daughter's dinosaur
pictures from the fridge. (This last led to some questions).

Alone one Saturday, while his wife took little Caoimhe
to hockey practice, he fed the shredder their title deeds,

sundry photographs, her birthday card archive and their U2 ticket
                                                            stubs,
twenty-five designer ties and a dozen from Dunnes that choked it.

He walked out in his shirt sleeves through the housing estate, past
the half-built semi-d's, over the waste ground and into the woods,
                                                            pushing

for days uphill toward its tangled centre, even as the path was
                                                        swallowed
by brambles, nettle-nests and dried-out twisted sycamores,

trying to ignore the thorns that rent and reddened his trousers,
foot-blisters, his stomach's whines, the topless and scrawny children

flickering in the undergrowth, the grey skin stretched over
their sloped, long foreheads, the way they moved, their giggling.

Section 9: Creative Problem Solving

Candidates have ten minutes to complete this section.

For each pair of statements indicate the one that best describes your attitude to problem solving. (Circle the 'X' or 'Y' in each case).

Candidates will answer every question.

X Sometimes the most effective or creative solutions come to me when I am not actually thinking about the problem at hand.
Y While the problem solving process is incomplete I find it difficult to relax.

X I often feel guilty about not getting enough accomplished.
Y I feel it is important to take as much time as is necessary to deal with any given task.

X I find that playing the 'devil's advocate' when problem solving can be helpful.
Y In certain high-pressure situations I feel it is better to act immediately than to waste time examining every option.

X I look for quality not quantity when 'brainstorming'.
Y I tend to avoid making decisions based on 'gut feelings' or intuition.

X I find that exploring eccentric ideas is usually a waste of time.
Y When working on a problem I enjoy thinking outside the box.

X I respect tradition but it is important that we are not afraid of change.
Y The first step in the problem-solving process is to examine the situation in the light of past experience, I have found that it is often best to stick with what works.

X In general, once I have reached a decision I feel good about it.

Y I sometimes need others to reassure me that I have made a good decision.

X I have found that throwing out old assumptions at the start of the problem-solving process is naïve.

Y I would prefer to work with a creative rather than with a careful person.

X I have difficulty narrowing things down when immersed in the decision-making process (I see *too* many different possible solutions/approaches).

Y If my suggestions are rejected I sometimes feel embarrassed or ashamed.

X I tend to stop generating possible solutions once I've found one that is likely to work.

Y I believe the best decision is one that can easily be changed.

X As a general rule I am always on the lookout for new ways to approach a problem.

Y I am suspicious of change for the sake of change; sometimes it is better to stick with the status quo.

X When brainstorming I find it essential to stop and think critically about suggestions.

Y I often feel that time is running out and there is too much left to do.

Pornography

Just before they upgraded the crime scene
they took the half-naked body to storage

in a blacked-out Volvo (as the evening darkened
like bruise-skin and turned bruise-orange

at its edges), past concerned locals, forensics
from Dublin, the resting crew of the Sky News helicopter,

Gardaí in their high-vis vests, through a hydra
of microphones and a rolling maul of photographers

that made me think of Cantona's one-liner
about the gulls and the herring ships,

past a yellowing van not far back in the shadows,
hooked up to an uncertain generator, selling chips.

Black Noise

Black noise has been described as an 'aural shadow'
or 'sonic after-image', or, memorably, as 'a mingled blizzard

of second-hand voices'. It is a ghost that wanders darkly through
the chambers of the ear forever, once listened to never to be
                                                    unheard.

Take this woman: late twenties, gray tracksuit, longish hair.
She has come, for whatever reason, to this sheltered bay,

her steps recorded perfectly in its damp and yielding sand
as she power-walks along the tide-line. This is the best part of her day,

she thinks, as the wind fiddles with her blown, black hair
and she stares out at the metallic, unrippled surface of the sea.

Even here, however, those shades of sound continue.
Though she is quite alone, she can hear it faintly,

the black noise, behind the swash and backwash
of those tender waves that scarcely disturb the shingle:

it is a hiss blended from Hanover Street kangos
and the nightly rumba of the washing machine, from every
                                                    insidious jingle

off the breakfast show, from ring tones and ohrwurmen
and the sullen humming of the office AC. She angles her head but
                                                    it's still there,

staining the water's insistent sibilance, the haranguing of the gulls,
sursurant, repetitive, no longer in the ear.

Breaking Even

Lower Basin Street, 17.05.02

'The apartment blocks were stubby, tobacco-stained fingers. There was this kid in the drizzle hurling. I heard him before I saw him, the sliotar's hollow *thwock* echoing through the empty yard. There was just shit everywhere, man; empties, what might have been syringes, a rusting upturned bicycle. I mean it wasn't raining like it does in Florida but it was coming down pretty heavy and, dude, I'm telling you this guy was wearing nothing, just jeans and some kind of T-shirt. He was, like, thirteen or fourteen I guess. There was something almost attractive in the way his body flicked and twisted, in his canine scrawniness. His skin was like a shower curtain, beaded with water and almost see-through. It was one of those moments, Kelly... I could have...He was still there, taking aim, I kid you not, over and over again at a sodden election poster. The buildings' shadows...I really felt something.'

CREDIT

Gruel, 17.05.02

A joke archive, a grainy video about somebody's father,
dresses that were commissioned by BT2,

photographic self-portraits by a big-titted Swede,
brown envelopes that held nothing but an IOU,

and our young adulthood in their many colours
(but mainly black): 'I just *adore*
Caiomhe's new stuff'…'my third opening this week'…
'sort of; the critic as host'…

I sipped salty wine, dreading the mention of insurance
or house prices, of *Friends* or the word 'post',

and thought of the spilt milk and the money spent,
our wastefulness, of all the possibilities we were sure to miss

and of course did. Will someone mention the fucking *election*?
We might have been otherwise. We were and are like this.

I raised my glass to Dame Street beyond the window,
to the fine diners scuttling through the rain, to wealth

and German engineering, to the rain-lashed ATM queue, the pubs,
the Chinese girl sprinting in her Subway uniform. Your health.

Southern Shores

to Eve

To your tiny ears my words make no more sense
than static, or management-babble,
or out-of-tune Chinese,
as you waddle down the beach beside me
your fragile hand in mine
over sand that is almost hot enough to scald.

We step gingerly past an old couple
stretched out on a picnic blanket
(licking sand-coated ice cream
and listening to a match)
and two bikini'd teenagers playing netless tennis

toward the ocean that offers us
a winking invite.

But up close, despite the sun,
it's freezing of course, and oddly grey,
and seaweed bobs up here and there
in colourful clumps.

But it dowses our toes, Eve,
and logs us into the ancient systems
of water's flows and evaporations,

       that joins this ice-water lapping our ankles,
       with the rain that greases the hungry doors
       and stains the grey graffitied gables
       and rusts the car-skeletons
       in the tenement estates
       of Moyross and Knocknaheeney.

that connects these shallows we jink and high-step through
with the haze rising from the look-out towers
of the silos rusting in Kazakhstan
manned by underpaid Asiatic soldiers
in hand-me-down Soviet regalia.

that binds this tide now up to my knees
with the perspiration in the inner jungle
that forms in beads on the fur of the monkey
with the yellow fang and the filthy blood,

that links each weedy wave darkening my shorts
with the Evian chilling at the marketing quarterly.

I could tell you the monsters are not real
though you wouldn't, of course, understand
and besides these four horsemen will not pass by.

Yet on the off-chance that words could spell out
some charm to protect you,
to gird you a little against what will come,
or even against the everyday difficulties,
let me wish you privacy:

I want to give you silence and darkness
not the city's glare and clang.

I want your name to slip free of the databases.

I want these stanzas to be a cove of words,
a shelter from the syrupy tide
of slogans and strap-lines
that daily washes over you.

As you cling to me
I trudge out further
past reptilian lengths and punk hair-dos
that slowly bob past us
and black things like webs.

Gabriel's Waltz

It is said that the philtrum, or indentation between the centre of the nostrils and the lip, is caused by the finger of the angel Gabriel as he comforts each child on his or her entrance into the world.

Sssh. My finger on your lips,
my finger tracing your tears,
is not quite enough
to shush you up

as you whimper,
as you sob out your terror
at these strange shores you've surfaced on.

It's as if you can already sense the barbarians
that lurk behind bushes,
at the head of the classroom,
like wraiths down back alleyways,
and behind neighbourly faces.

Right now you're just a bundle of futures,
all of them featuring somebody's hands,
whiteness, sneezes, alarms that scream
for attention, stray light, sleep's mud bath,
a corn-coloured dress among the barley,
a piano, abandonment, light collapsing.

Let's get it clear from day one that you're here
for life. All that's uncertain
is the long or the short of it.

And may you not leave as you entered,
in a hospital ward in the dead of night
after panting and hard labour...

Hush. Stop whining now.
It's just headlights slanting through the window,
the night-nurse yawning on her rounds.
A door slams in the corridor.

Machines beep. Welcome home.

After Words

1

I could have sworn that it was him the other night,
half-cut and ancient, in a pillar of lamplight,
his shrivelled face twitching beneath his Trilby
as he gawped at the girls squatting and vomiting
in the alleys behind the night-club. *Why did I blacken
so many pages, so many pristine unyielding squares?*
he must have thought, as he listened to the couple
rutting in the closed-down chip-shop's doorway.
Why did I lend my best years to the silence?
He jostled through the Four Star Pizza queue,
side-stepped an embryonic, drunken scuffle
and skulked into the solidifying mist that spangled
his glasses, his oversized 20's raincoat
of no particular colour.

2

My windows are thin
as the flimsiest paper.
They cannot preserve the silences

that flourish when our mouths connect
from the teeming hubbub of the clubbers
disgorged into Hanover Street.

I hear the girls keening theatrically,
vodka sobbing,
and the slap-happy banter

of the check-shirted boys.
It is the sound of a schoolyard, of frustration.
I listen for the rage in their brittle hilarity.

Her body beside me
is white as can be
imagined in this city of stains,

as Prague after snowfall
on a Czech dusk in December,
unblemished as the empty page.

Printed in the United Kingdom
by Lightning Source UK Ltd.
120465UK00001B/7-54